Endorsements

"I am a big believer in 90-day planning, and in their new book, *Build Leadership Momentum: How to Create the Perfect Principal Entry Plan*, Daniel Bauer and Ariel Curry map out a practical framework for the first 90 days of the school year. Not only is this book engagingly written, but it offers a unique and imminently more practical approach to starting the school year on the right foot—one that takes into consideration not only the work of the principal, but the principal as a person.

"Daniel Bauer's unique perspective and practical approach is something I wish I'd had when I first became an administrator. He cuts through the noise of the endless to-dos most new principals face and helps you focus on what matters most."

Robyn R. Jackson, Ph.D., CEO of Mindsteps Inc., podcaster, and author of international best-seller *Never Work Harder Than Your Students*

"Danny Bauer has created an incredibly relevant, powerful, easy to read book that helps principals do the work they need to do and do it with greater ease and enthusiasm. Looking at an administrator's job from five angles, Bauer's book supports readers with really useful scaffolds and tools. With the help of this book, and the work you will put in as a result, one can start the school year with less stress and more productivity. A win for everyone."

Jennifer Abrams, communications consultant, leadership coach, and author of *Having Hard Conversations*

"A handbook that every leader should have to start the school year and build positive momentum! This book is practical, to the point, and has information that can be gleaned by leaders with any level of experience or expertise in the field. It is packed with 'ah ha!' moments, guides and tools, and the reality checks some of us leaders may need to ensure we are not only taking care of ourselves but also the staff and students of our school community."

Vince Bustamante, consultant and co-author of *Leader Ready: Four Pathways to Prepare Aspiring School Leaders* and *Great Teaching by Design: From Intention to Implementation in the Visible Learning Classroom*

"He's done it again—but even better! Danny has proven time and again that there are specific strategies that can help leaders improve. This book takes it even further by providing a plan for building leaders as they start their journey so everything else becomes easier as they continue. This book contains the answer to the question every leader asks each year: How do I make the largest possible positive impact while protecting my personal life?

"*Build Leadership Momentum* doesn't just tell you how; it shows you. True to Danny's style of over-delivering, it is full of templates, strategies, and resources to further develop yourself as an impactful leader. This book should live on the desk of every leader who is committed to continually improving their school 90 days at a time."

Dr. Christopher Jones, principal, speaker, podcast host, and author of *SEEing to Lead: Support. Engage. Empower.*

"Being a principal is tough. There are many books written about theory, but few that give you a 90-day, step-by-step plan. Danny has given us a quick read to walk into day one with a plan on what to do, so leaders can give more attention to the 'surprises' that aren't in any book *ever*."

Dr. CJ Lowery, assistant superintendent and certified Professional Ruckus Maker

"Danny is setting you up for success in this book. He takes the common sense 'do now' ideas that we may know and shares how to make them a reality in our leadership. He helps us remember to care for self and then fill the buckets of those we serve. Great reference and toolkit for us to use for the greater good!"

Michael Lubelfeld, Ed.D., superintendent and co-author of *The Unfinished Leader: A School Leadership Framework for Growth and Development*

"One of the great asks in providing effective professional development for principals is the demand for less theory and more practical leadership strategies. Through the provision of high impact processes, tools, and necessary actions, this book will excite and motivate principals to successfully plan for and navigate the myriad challenges inherent to the role! It is a must read for all school leaders!"

Dr. Tim Cusack, superintendent and co-author of *Leader-Ready: Four Pathways to Prepare Aspiring School Leaders*

"This book is an invaluable resource for new principals who want to hit the ground running and establish themselves as effective leaders in their schools. Bauer provides practical, actionable advice on everything from building relationships with staff and students to creating a positive culture for the school.

"What I appreciate most about this book is its holistic approach to leadership. The authors recognize that effective principals have a clear entry plan, allowing them to collaboratively lay the groundwork for building a culture of learning and growth that supports students, teachers, and staff.

"In short, this is a must-read for any new principal wanting to positively impact their school. I highly recommend this book to anyone looking to create a successful entry plan and build strong, sustainable leadership momentum."

Evan Robb, principal, speaker, and author of *Aiming High: Leadership Actions to Increase Learning Gains*

"Danny Bauer's genius is in combining both relentless optimism and fine-tuned systems. This book is one more example of that genius at work. I'm eager to share it with my own principal."

Dave Stuart Jr., teacher and author of *The Will to Learn: Cultivating Student Motivation Without Losing Your Own*

"In *Build Leadership Momentum*, Daniel and Ariel have given me the inspiration to look forward to the next school year, even as a principal for 24 years! Every summer of my life is filled with anxiety as I worry about solutions to building a better school culture and establishing strong relationships with my staff, students, and families. But I have found the perfect principal entry plan, and I am ready to lead and live better than ever! If you are a principal who wants to make an impact right away, or plan to become one, read this book twice!"

Salome Thomas-EL, Ed.D., award-winning principal, speaker, and author

"This is a planning tool for now and for years to come. The intentionality of 'best self' is foundational in the planning. I always think I'm going to take care of myself, but that is the first thing that is dismissed when I become overwhelmed. The pacing is very attainable, I value the suggestions for the timing of the implementation, and the resources that are described and provided are essential for lifting this plan.

"Our district recently completed a process to identify our core values, and they are quality education, integrity, and communication. I was able to see in each section where I/we can take action and set the tone for living out these core values. It's time to take action!"

Stacey Green, elementary/middle school principal and #RuckusMaker

"What a fantastic book and a must-read for everyone, from those new to school leadership to seasoned veterans who have been leading the charge for years! As we ease out of the pandemic, this is the right book at the right time. Danny skillfully provides an actionable plan to transform the school year in just 90 days.

"Every school leader I have had the privilege of working with has described the excitement and trepidation that permeate the start of each new school year. There is simply too much for a leader to consider and get right as they prepare for the year—that is, unless they have a proven plan to follow.

"If school leaders put into action the entry plan carefully outlined in this book, the stress they are used to carrying into the school year will vanish. Instead, they will start with the same sense of ease that July brings while knowing the plan they have put in place will set their teachers and students up for success."

Mitch Weathers, founder and CEO of Organized Binder

Build Leadership Momentum

How to Create the Perfect Principal Entry Plan

Daniel Bauer

WITH ARIEL CURRY

Foreword by Peter DeWitt

RUCKUS
MAKER
M E D I A

ISBN 979-8-9881350-0-5 (paperback) | ISBN 979-8-9881350-1-2 (ebook)

First publication: 2023

This book is dedicated to all the Ruckus Makers designing the future of school right now.

Contents

Foreword

When I interviewed for my role as a school principal, I was in front of a panel of 17 people, including parents, teachers, a board member, the school superintendent, and my predecessor, who was going to become the assistant superintendent. There were some uncomfortable moments, like when one of the parents, who had two children in the school, began sobbing because she was going to miss my predecessor so much. But overall, I remember a feeling of calm even though I had to sit and answer questions for over an hour.

As I handed them my teaching portfolio in a very large binder, I told them that although I did not have any leadership experience, I wanted them to see what kind of teacher I had been over the past 11 years. I hoped that would help them get a sense of my values so they could focus and connect with me as a human. It clearly worked because I got the job.

It was April, and I did not officially begin my role until July. Although I was teaching in another school district, my predecessor invited me to come over to the school any time I wanted. Once a week, I would leave the school where I was teaching at 3:30 and make the 30-minute drive to the school I would lead so I could meet teachers, talk with the principal, and greet the students who were in the afterschool program.

The secretary handed me a yearbook and told me to study the pictures of students and teachers so I would know their names when I saw them. Just like studying for a college exam, I studied the yearbook, and I was able to remember names when I met the people in person. That was the extent of the training and preparation that I received before becoming responsible for the academics, culture, communication, and operations in my school.

As leaders, the only time we get to talk about who we are as leaders is during interviews for the job. After that, we seem to fall into the daily grind. This book is an opportunity for you to pause and consider who you are as a leader. Why does that matter? It's simple. Leaders who have self-awareness and seek feedback from a group of diverse thinkers are more likely to be successful in their role.

I was fortunate as a leader because my predecessor and the teachers, parents, students, and staff wanted me to be successful. My first year was filled with opportunities to observe how different people collaborated, and how teachers engaged students. I went to every classroom every morning to say good morning to the students and teachers, and then I circled back to watch learning taking place.

Despite what you may have heard, leadership is not about going to the dark side; it is very much an opportunity to build relationships, foster growth in students and adults, and collaborate with people so you can find your best ideas as a group, not just as an individual.

This book provides you the space to consider what your actions will be for your first 90 days as a principal. It gives you the opportunity to think through who you *want* to be as a leader—not just who you think you *have* to be as a leader.

As you go from page to page and engage in the reflections, consider not only what you are thinking, but also consider why you are thinking in that way. Those metacognitive moments will help you strengthen your leadership.

As I navigated my way through the first 90 days before I was even officially in the role, and then the next 90 days after that, and then the years that went by, there was one thought I had repeatedly: *I am so fortunate to be a school leader.* I was grateful for the role and the community, even during the tough times, but I was also proud to lead.

As you read the pages and develop your 90-day entry plan, please consider where gratitude fits in, and make sure that whatever you decide to do within that plan are learning moves that you can actually commit to. Make sure those actions focus on learning and growth, not just for students and other adults, but for yourself as well.

Peter DeWitt, Ed.D., author of *Collaborative Leadership: Six Influences That Matter Most*

Introduction

Better Than Fantasy

It happened every year like clockwork.

July was incredible. Sometimes I slept in, or I got up early to go on a run and then relax with a cup of coffee. I caught up on my favorite science fiction/fantasy book series and met my wife at her office for lunch.

I went into the school a couple times a week to interview new staff, create our master schedules, and take care of logistical operations. There were the annual back-to-school professional development (PD) days to organize and lead and new teacher orientation meetings to plan. But for the most part, July felt like a much-needed escape.

Until August.

I felt it creeping up on me as I watched the calendar days disappear one after the other. The anxiety. I tried to ignore it for as long as possible, pushing off that inevitable day in mid-August when I would be overloaded and overwhelmed with a mile-long list of issues and to-dos that all needed to get done yesterday. The first day of school always seemed to come sooner than I was ready for.

Don't get me wrong; there was excitement, too. I couldn't wait to see the kids and my staff (most of them, anyway). I looked forward to getting everyone else excited about the start of school. I lived off of their enthusiasm, trying to soak up enough energy and momentum to get me at least to winter break without burning out.

Why did it seem like something *always* went wrong at the start of the new school year? There was always a medical emergency, a discipline issue, a district miscommunication, an angry parent, a bus schedule off track. With having to put out fires from the get-go, I felt off-balance right from the start. I just hoped I could make it through the first 90 days without collapsing.

The truth is, I was never really ready for the beginning of a new school year. No one taught me how to prepare myself for it. There were no principal PD days to attend, no principal handbook I could read that would give me the play-by-play for getting the school year off to a good start. Once I became a principal, it was sink or swim. And for many years, I sank.

I'm guessing you've been there, too.

Every school leader hopes for the best at the start of the school year. If you're an optimist like I am, you probably view those first 90 days as a fresh start, a chance for everything to go right. You envision students walking (not running, like my middle schoolers did) calmly to their classrooms, teachers getting along and turning in grades on time, parents showering you with flowers as you walk into the building...Ok, maybe not that. We'll leave the fantasy to the pros.

But you definitely don't envision the chaos that always sneaks its way into the school building every year. You hope and say a prayer and dive back into *The Hitchhiker's Guide to the Galaxy*, wondering in the back of your mind if you could hitchhike your way back to July.

The Problem With Hope Alone

The problem we all discover very quickly each year is that hope is not a strategy. That saying is cliché for a reason. It's true: Hope helps us when we're communicating our vision for the future and creating a culture that people want to be a part of (We'll talk about that more in Chapters 2 and 3). And hope is the birthplace of ideas. But hope can't prevent the last-minute mix-ups or kids getting sick in the hallway trashcan or a particularly bad summer slide of kids' learning retention.

I like to tell leaders: "Ideas are great, but not the greatest."

What's better than an idea? Action.

Hope without action is meaningless.

The good news is that hope is not the only tool available to you.

No, you probably didn't receive a lot of training for your current role. You might not feel supported or prepared for the task ahead of you. You might think it'll take years to adjust to the back-to-school rhythm and be able to pull it off successfully. But here's the thing: You're not alone, you're more ready than you think you are, and you don't have to wait years before you can head into a new school year with confidence and clarity.

In this book, I'm going to show you how to eliminate the back-to-school anxiety by creating the perfect 90-day entry plan for success and executing it with style.

The Perfect 90-Day Entry Plan

Imagine that instead of the first day of school feeling like a runaway train headed toward disaster (and you're just praying it doesn't go off the rails), you could start the school year feeling ready and confident to handle whatever comes your way. Imagine that your staff and students were clear on expectations and knew exactly how they could contribute toward helping the school meet its goals.

Imagine that the peace and authentic joy you felt in July didn't stop on August 1. Imagine that you had enough time and space to keep reading your favorite book *during* the school year.

This *is* possible with the right kind of entry plan.

We usually think of entry plans as tools for principals who are new to a school—their own, self-guided "new principal orientation" to help them get settled in a new building with new teachers and students.

And they are.

But I believe every principal should have an entry plan that they can use every year, no matter how long they've been leading that particular school.

Having a 90-day entry plan will help you:

- Get clarity on how you want to start the school year.

- Set the tone for the culture that you want to see.

- Create meaningful relationships with your colleagues.

- Learn how to communicate more effectively.

- And get more done in 90 days than your colleagues get done in a year.

Let's look at a quick example of how one principal got off the merry-go-round of chaos and started down a calmer, more strategic path. John Unger is the principal at West Fork Middle School in West Fork, Arkansas. For several years, back to school was a hectic time. He and his leadership team tried to stay organized by holding countless meetings and creating detailed agendas—sometimes up to 15 pages long!—but still felt they lacked focus.

John was up at night with worries like, *Who's in charge of what? What are our office manager's duties? Does everyone have their agendas? Is the schedule ready?* Then, when school actually started, he and his team quickly became distracted extinguishing fires and handling logistical issues that came up.

While listening to the Better Leaders Better Schools™ podcast one summer, John heard about the Back-to-School Challenge I was hosting for which the goal was to create a 90-day entry plan to start the year off well. He joined the Ruckus Maker Nation online community to participate in the five-day challenge. His number one goal was to learn how to focus his team on doing the right work at the right time.

Throughout the challenge, John learned about the five buckets of the plan, which helped him think more strategically about how to organize and streamline his team's efforts in those first 90 days. We'll learn more about John's story in the coming chapters, but first, let's learn more about how the plan is organized.

There are five categories, or buckets as I call them, that you'll want to think about while we're creating your 90-day entry plan for the start of the school year. These five buckets will be the topics of the book's chapters:

Chapter 1: You—yes, you!

Leaders usually plan for themselves last, if they plan for themselves at all. Unfortunately, this self-sacrifice is praised and rewarded in our systems. Your tendency to put yourself last is likely what got you into your leadership role. But it's not going to sustain you or your school. If you are burning out under stress, you won't be able to serve the people in your school community. You cannot give from an empty cup.

So in this book, we're not leaving self-care up to chance. Your plan to take care of yourself is integral to achieving success in the first 90 days. We're going to make a plan for you *first*. We'll also talk about how to refine the values that define your leadership, how to avoid your idea enemies, and how to show up the way you want to for the people in your school community.

Chapter 2: Communication

After carefully planning how you want to show up as a leader, we will look at your communication systems next because, without thoughtful and intentional planning for communication, nothing else you try to accomplish in the first 90 days will be successful.

Chapter 3: Academics

Learning is the business of school; it's what we're here to facilitate for our students. Yet there are so many ways learning happens. If we spread our attention and effort too thin across all of the possible areas that could be improved, we won't make an impact anywhere.

This chapter will guide you through a process of inquiry to help keep you and your team focused on the improvements that will have the greatest impact.

Chapter 4: Culture

Often, the first 90 days of school are so filled with logistical worries and problem-solving that we neglect to think about the intangibles: the energy and feel of the school as well as the health and safety of the learning environment. We focus on the alligator closest to the boat and hope that when we fix that problem, everything else will fall into place.

Hopefully you're seeing a pattern here. Nothing happens by chance—even our school's culture; we have to thoughtfully plan for it. I believe in visualization and meditation—two important tools that help us create a vision and goals for our schools. In Chapter 4, we'll discuss how to employ them to establish priorities and foster a healthy school environment.

Chapter 5: Operations

Most school leaders are tempted to focus on operations first—the schedules, policies, facilities, and procedures—but you'll notice that in our 90-day plan, operations comes *last*. Yes, operations is the setting in place of systems for the first four buckets, but without knowing what those buckets are, you can't establish your systems.

In Chapter 5, we can start to pay attention to the logistical issues and make a plan for solving problems when they arise.

Chapter 6: Your Plan

Finally, in Chapter 6, we'll bring together all of the ideas from the first five chapters to give you a template you can use to create your own perfect entry plan.

Why 90 Days?

Ninety days works because it's not so far into the future that you can procrastinate and avoid taking action. It's also not so soon that you'll think your plan is unrealistic. It's just the right length for you to start to see real measurable progress right away.

What I've found from coaching hundreds of school leaders like you through this plan is that 90 days is the *perfect* amount of time to get to work and do something special. Don't believe me? Test it out. Verify the claim for yourself.

So, Ruckus Maker, what do you say?

I can't promise it'll be better than the fantasy book you've been eyeing on your bookshelf. But I *can* promise this story has a happy ending.

Are you ready?

Let's get started.

Take Action: Your Day 91 Vision

Don't start writing your 90-day plan yet! Instead, take some time today to think and write about this prompt:

Imagine it's Day 91 into the new school year, and you've executed on the plan we're creating in this book. You're thrilled with the progress that you see around you. What does that progress look like in your school? How are you measuring it?

Chapter 1

Bring Your Best Self to School

How often did you eat lunch last school year?

And I don't mean the times you scarfed down a microwaved burrito while answering emails or running from one building to the other. I mean, how often did you sit down (ideally outside) to eat a healthy meal without any distractions or outside responsibilities weighing on you?

If you roll your eyes or laugh out loud at the idea of being able to eat that kind of lunch, this chapter is for you. Because you deserve to eat a lunch like that every single day.

Of course, this isn't just about lunch. The time and space you have to eat lunch is indicative of the overall margin you have in your work life and the stress you might be experiencing at school.

EdSurge reported that the mental health and wellbeing of principals has been particularly low since the onset of the COVID-19 pandemic (Sullivan, 2022). And a 2022 study conducted by the RAND Corporation found that 85 percent of principals report experiencing job-related stress (Steiner et al., 2022).

But I don't need to tell you that. You see it everyday. Forget about lunch; we're barely sleeping and making it through the day!

It's easy for us to excuse the amount of stress on our shoulders; we think about the mile-long list of things that need to get done and the constant demands on our time. Shouldn't the other people in our school building come first?

Of course we have to think about the other people in our buildings. In the foreword to Simon Sinek's 2014 book *Leaders Eat Last*, Lieutenant General George J. Flynn wrote, "Great leaders truly care about those they are privileged to lead and understand that the true cost of the leadership privilege comes at the expense of self-interest" (p. xii).

Sinek wrote his book in response to the cultural lack of trust he saw in the businesses he worked with. Over and over again, he saw leaders take advantage of others and prioritize themselves over the people they were supposed to be serving.

That's not the problem I see in schools. I see, and the research agrees, that we have the *opposite* problem in education. Leaders are burning out and leaving schools at an alarming rate, not by choice but for the sake of pure survival. That constant churn—the continual turnover of leadership—is harmful to our schools. Not to mention, it's harmful to you.

I know, I know, you picked up this book to create a 90-day entry plan for your school. But I've learned over several years of helping Ruckus Makers like yourself that if you are not healthy, your school won't be healthy. This is why the motto for Better Leaders Better Schools™ is "When YOU get better, everyone wins."

The most neglected factor of school success is *you*. When school starts, it's easy to get sidetracked by all of the other buckets that feel more important and more urgent than taking care of ourselves.

So in this chapter, we'll talk about how you can plan to show up as your best self in the first 90 days.

The Ruckus Maker Mindset Tool

In 2018, John Antulov was waiting for his wife, Trish, to come home. Trish was the principal of a school in Perth, Australia, and it wasn't uncommon for her to stay late into the evenings to get work done. He wasn't too worried about it until she missed his phone calls. That was unlike her. By 10 p.m., John was seriously concerned, and he went to the school to check on her.

He found that Trish had died at her desk (Hiatt, 2018).

This is a dramatic and, thankfully, uncommonly tragic story. But it's a good cautionary tale for all of us who want to be around for a long time to serve our school communities.

Ruckus Makers want to be top performers, and all top performers work hard. That's a fact. But the best top performers know how to recuperate and rest as well so that they can put in the hard work.

I like to use a simple self-evaluation with the leaders I coach to help them prioritize their mental and physical health. The Ruckus Maker Mindset Tool™ looks at five key indicators:

- **Eating**, because, like any high performer, you need to be putting the right fuel in your body;

- **Sleeping**, because our bodies need time to rest and recharge for optimal performance;

- **Moving**, because it's easier to maintain momentum when we move consistently;

- **Meditating**, because our minds need time and space to process information and function optimally; and

- **Unplugging**, because it's hard to do any of the above things if we're being constantly interrupted.

On a scale of 1 to 5—with 1 being "This area in my life sucks right now," and 5 being "I am rocking this area!"—rate yourself in each domain:

Eating: ____

Sleeping: ____

Moving: ____

Meditating: ____

Unplugging: ____

If you're reading this before the start of the school year (as I hope you are!), then I hope that you're doing great in all five of these domains. But if you're struggling before the school year has even started, that's an indicator that this area of your life needs your full attention *now* before the busyness of school begins.

Take a few minutes to brainstorm specific ways you can take care of yourself in each of these domains. Here are some questions to reflect on:

Eating:

- What kinds of snacks can you eat throughout the day?

- When will you eat lunch?

- What will you eat for lunch?

- How will you prepare food so that you're able to eat consistently nutritious meals?

Sleeping:

- What time will you start getting ready for bed?

- What routines and rituals can you establish to prepare for sleep?

- What time do you want to wake up in the morning?

Moving:

- What are your favorite types of movement?

- How can you find time to move throughout the day at school?

- What kinds of exercise can you incorporate into your weekly routine?

Meditating:

- When is the best time for you to meditate?

- Where can you meditate that is quiet and free of distractions?

- Will you use guided meditations, music, or silence to help you quiet your mind?

Unplugging:

- Where will you keep your phone while you unplug?

- What steps can your faculty and students take before trying to reach you?

- Who can be a point of contact for you while you're unplugging?

Practice the 85% Rule

Olympic runner Carl Lewis famously took a counterintuitive approach to winning the 100-meter dash. Unlike his competitors, Lewis held back at the beginning of the race, often trailing the other runners at the 40-meter mark. But as their energy began to flag in the last half or quarter of the sprint, Lewis maintained a consistent pace and managed to come in first, winning nine Olympic gold medals with what would become known as the 85% rule. *Inc.* contributor Jeff Haden (2020) wrote that Lewis trusted "that preparation and technique—not 'extra' effort in this moment—would pay off."

Practicing the 85% rule means that, at all times, you're consistently using just 85% of your energy. The hardest part about this is learning to *hold back*, even when you could give more. It feels awkward, uncomfortable, frustrating, even morally wrong at times—but it is the best strategy for consistently contributing with excellence and avoiding the danger of burning out.

Once you get in the habit of taking care of yourself so you can bring your best self to school, you can begin thinking about what actions you want to take and how the people in your building will experience you. We do that by defining our sticky core values and getting to know our idea enemies.

Define Your Sticky Core Values

Every leader should live by what I call sticky core values. These are ideas that guide our actions and decisions from day to day.

When we think of values, we tend to think of words like honesty, integrity, excellence, and dedication. Obviously, these are admirable qualities to hold. The problem with general terms like these, however, is that they don't provide a lot of guidance for our everyday actions.

A more powerful approach to defining values is to embrace memorable phrases that illustrate how you want to show up as a leader in your community every day. Here are my sticky core values to give you an idea:

Turn Pro

In everything I do, I want to show up to do my best, no matter how I feel. I put aside my complaints and focus on the job in front of me because that's what the pros do. According to author Steven Pressfield, this is the *only* way to beat what he calls The Resistance and what you may know as imposter syndrome.

Purple Cow

This is an idea from a book by Seth Godin (2004) of the same title: *Purple Cow: Transform Your Business by Being Remarkable.* I grew up driving the incredibly boring interstates in Illinois. There's nothing to see along these highways but cornfields and cows. And there are only two kinds of cows in Illinois: brown and white, or black and white.

Imagine, though, that you were driving along one day and saw a purple cow! You'd never forget it, right?

What's more—you'd tell everyone else about it.

My purple-cow value encourages me to seek out and create extraordinary experiences that others will never forget and that they will want to share with everyone they meet.

Ripple Effect

My focus is on long-term impact. I want my actions to have positive consequences not just now, but long into the future. I believe that small changes add up to big results over time. Therefore, in my decision making, I'm always asking myself what the ripple effects of this decision will be.

Forest From the Trees

I try to maintain a long-term perspective, which helps me with my ripple-effect value as well. It's easy to get caught up in minutiae, but I challenge myself to see the big picture of any situation.

Sponge That Scales

The idea of being a lifelong learner is a nice buzzword in education, but like all buzzwords, it tends to lose its value and meaning over time. Instead, I like the idea of being a sponge that scales because as I learn, my impact and influence grows. Like a sponge, I expand. This value not only tells me that I should be learning, but that I should be using and applying what I learn.

What are your sticky core values?

Know Your Idea Enemies

Your enemies are not the people you interact with; they're the ideas that hold you back. Think of them as the opposites of your sticky core values. These are the ideas that prevent you from making good decisions and showing up as your best self.

My enemies are:

Status Quo

Traditions can be good and useful, but often, they hold me back. I never want to let inertia or "the way we've always done things" keep me from innovating or creating those purple-cow experiences.

Stagnation

I think of stagnation as a lack of desire to learn and get better. Often I use busyness to productively procrastinate on the real work I should be doing, the work of learning and growing. Ironically, stagnation can be the highest in those who look like they're doing the most.

Isolation

Working and trying to lead on my own is a recipe for low performance. Business coach and author Greg Salciccioli (2011) says that isolation is the number one enemy of excellence. No one can get better in a vacuum.

Lack of Mentorship

I believe I need people who are at least 10 percent ahead of me to help me get where I want to go. Without that mentorship and guidance, I flounder. This enemy is one of the core reasons I've created the Better Leaders Better Schools™ administrator masterminds—so that leaders will never be without a mentor. I also make it a habit to surround myself with good mentors.

Open-Door Policies

While it's important to be available and present to the people in my school (and we'll discuss this more in Chapter 4), having an open-door policy is a terrible idea! Why? Because it invites distraction.

Most leaders with an open-door policy say something to the effect of: "People over paperwork." But what they really mean is: "I prioritize people over paperwork while at school. By doing so, however, I prioritize my work over time for myself and time for my family because I believe work is more important."

Ouch.

I cannot take care of myself when I am constantly distracted.

You might have similar enemies in your life, or you may encounter others. Your enemies might change over time. But know them and study them so that you're ready to do battle with them when they arise.

Take Action: Your Sticky Core Values

What are five phrases that describe how you want to show up at school? You might find inspiration for your sticky core values in books or from mentors in your life.

As you find phrases that resonate with you, list them here:

1. _____

2. _____

3. _____

4. _____

5. _____

What you stand for is important, but at times, knowing what you stand against can be even more impactful. What are the idea enemies you want to avoid?

1. _____

2. _____

3. _____

4. _____

5. _____

Chapter 2

Communicate How Much You Care

There's one thing that high-performing schools tend to have in common: good communication. Communication is how we facilitate everything else that we want to accomplish as a school community: our academics (which we'll discuss in the next chapter), our culture (Chapter 4), and our operations (Chapter 5).

On the other hand, when communication breaks down, the damage tends to extend to these other areas, too. It's important that we get this right if we want everything else to go well.

The biggest communication challenge that educators face is that we tend to have the wrong focus. We view communication as a checklist of district mandates and protocols from the central office that we need to pass along to our teachers and staff. Sure, we try to make it engaging—perhaps we sprinkle in a well-timed joke that no one laughs at—but that doesn't change the fact that we're trying to get through a laundry list of information, and everyone knows it.

If you're thinking this sounds familiar, you might realize that this is exactly what we tend to do to students, too—viewing education as a list of standards to force-feed into their brains. It's not effective for students, and it's not effective for our staff.

When we do try to deliver this information during staff or department meetings, we tend to get sidetracked by another challenge: a focus on ourselves. We're all human, and we're all highly sensitive to the way we're being perceived by the people around us.

Are they listening? Am I being funny enough? Do I have spinach in my teeth? So-and-so didn't say hi to me. Why hasn't you-know-who shown up yet? Is she ignoring me? This inner monologue distracts us from focusing on the people in front of us.

Remember the old adage: "People don't care how much you know until they know how much you care"?

It's cheesy, but it's true.

In the first 90 days, our primary goal is not to rush through a list of logistical to-dos or dominate the airwaves with our own plans and vision. It's to communicate how much we care.

And to do that, it helps to realign our ideas around who, what, where, and how we're communicating.

Who Is Communicating?

Communication has to flow two ways. Yes, as a leader we are responsible for communicating to our team. But in the back-to-school rush, we tend to forget that it's just as important, if not more important, for our team to be communicating with *us*.

Your focus, especially in the first 90 days, should be on listening and learning, not on dictating and informing. This is the best opportunity you'll have all year to get to know your team, to learn what's important to them, and to understand their pain points.

My favorite way to get to know my staff is to conduct a Get-to-Know-You Survey. Incorporate this survey into your back-to-school professional learning days; don't assign extra work for staff to do at home and cut into their precious remaining time before the school year starts. This small consideration shows them that you respect their out-of-school time, and it can provide a fun break from your typical back-to-school PD.

So what should go in your survey? These are the questions I encourage leaders to ask, but you might adjust these or create your own instead:

1. What do you want to know about your new principal?

2. What do you want me to know about you?

3. What is your favorite snack or treat?

4. What is your favorite song and who performs it?

5. When is your birthday?

6. Share three of your favorite traditions at [Name of Your School].

7. Share three strengths of [Name of Your School].

8. Share three opportunities for growth.

9. What challenges do we face as a school?

10. Who has been instrumental in shaping the school?

11. If you were me, what would you focus your attention on this year?

You can find a downloadable version of this survey on our website: buildleadershipmomentum.com.

Some of these questions might surprise you. They're not stale or typical; they're thoughtful and intriguing. Most importantly, they give you lots of fuel for integrating your team's personalities into your school communication throughout the rest of the year.

Think back to when you were a teacher. Imagine showing up to a weekly staff meeting to find your favorite snack food available or to hear your favorite song playing in the hallways. Maybe you even play a game with your team in which you guess whose favorite song is playing before a meeting. Imagine that your principal asked about your favorite hobby or asked if she could come cheer you on at your church's softball game.

This survey not only gives you significant information about what priorities you'll need to address throughout the year, it also gives your team a chance to get to know each other.

I always suggest that leaders make an effort to sit down with every staff member for at least 15 minutes in the first week of school. If you've already done the survey, these meetings are a chance for you to follow up on their responses or ask for further clarification.

It may not be with just staff that you need to improve communication. Principal John Unger's team at West Fork Middle School identified that there was a gap in communication between the school and parents, so they decided to create a family engagement committee. This group was responsible for making sure parents were in-the-know about important updates from the school and for planning events to create a stronger sense of community.

For John, the surprising upside to this initiative was that it took one more worry off his plate and allowed him to focus on other priorities.

What Is Being Communicated?

In the first 90 days, when you communicate to your staff, you should focus on communicating just two things: your vision for your school's success and how you plan to tackle their obstacles and challenges. Both should be rooted in how much you care.

Let's talk about vision first.

The Remarkable Vision Formula

In the Bible, the prophet, Habakkuk, was waiting for the Lord to answer him, and God said, "Write the vision, make it plain on tablets, so *he may run who reads it*." Our visions should not only be communicated plainly, but should be actionable and exciting so that those who read it can (and will want to) "run" with it.

How do we do that? With the Remarkable Vision Formula.

The Remarkable Vision Formula has three parts:

1. Remarkable Life

2. Remarkable Family

3. Remarkable School

Your Remarkable Vision starts with you—what is your dream for a Remarkable Life? We talked a lot about this in Chapter 1, but we need to keep asking ourselves:

- What fills my cup?

- What does it look like when my life is a 10 out of 10?

The next piece of your Remarkable Vision is a Remarkable Family. Often our family is where we find the most meaning and purpose in our lives. If things aren't going well at home, it tends to come with us to work.

To brainstorm a path toward your Remarkable Family, ask:

- What family issues or problems do I tend to take with me to work?

- What does it look like when my family is whole, happy, and healthy?

- How can I support my family members in being their best selves?

Finally, the last piece—and it's last for a reason—of your Remarkable Vision is a Remarkable School.

Ask yourself:

- In three years, what do I want students, staff, and parents to be saying about our school?

- What do I need to do on a day-to-day basis to achieve this vision?

You can't create your vision for a remarkable school in a vacuum, and you can't let others steer the vision away from your core values either. To find the right balance, draft the first iteration of your Remarkable School Vision on your own. Spend time in nature, go to your favorite weekend escape, or simply spend time journaling in your local coffee shop. Remove yourself from possible distractions so you can think deeply and dream big.

Then, invite your leadership team to send feedback. Make changes, and then circulate the vision to all of your department heads. Repeat the process, asking for feedback from broader concentric circles until everyone has had an opportunity to offer their input. You should end up with something that feels true to you *and* has everyone's buy-in.

You can find more information about these three components in my book, *Remarkable Vision Formula*.

Addressing Challenges

When you gather information through the Get-to-Know-You Survey, you'll learn what obstacles and challenges your team is facing. While you can't make everything a priority—as we'll discuss more in Chapter 3—taking the time to acknowledge and address your staff's concerns will show them how much you care.

What I recommend you do with your team is write down on index cards the top 10 key concerns you find in the survey. Keep these index cards somewhere close, perhaps in your office or wherever you do your planning, so you can reference them any time you're preparing for a staff meeting or drafting a newsletter.

If you can solve any of the challenges fairly easily, try to address those in the first month of school to show that you've heard your team and you're taking action right away.

Most likely, though, the challenges will be more complex and might be tied to factors outside of your control. For those, I suggest consistently reminding your team that their concerns are important to you and that you're keeping these challenges top of mind. Doing so will solve half the problem right away.

Where Are You Communicating?

This is the easy part of communication: the mediums we use for conveying our vision and addressing challenges. Already, we've mentioned team PD meetings and email newsletters. Other methods of communication include:

- Direct emails

- Classroom visits

- Parent communication

- Posters

- School app

- Texts

- Social media

- Video

There are many great books and online resources about how to effectively use these methods of communication, and as a sponge that scales, hopefully you are interested in taking advantage of those resources to level up your communication skills.

I see leaders who get trapped in thinking, *If I said it/communicated it once, they should have seen/heard it.* But people are busy. They're buried in tasks and to-dos just like you are. Be redundant in your communication.

If you say it in a staff meeting, put it in the newsletter, on the internal message board, and on social media. Ask yourself, *How many ways can I overcommunicate what's important so that people actually hear the message?* Jeff Weiner (2020), Executive Chairman of LinkedIn says, "You need to repeat yourself so often that you get sick of hearing yourself say it. And only then will people begin to internalize it."

Remember, though, that what matters most is not the tools you use; it's *how* you use them.

How Are You Communicating?

Your team will know how much you care when you take the time to build trust. In a study of organizational trust, leadership consultants Jack Zenger and Joseph Folkman (2019) showed that three factors contribute to the level of trust people have in their leaders:

- Positive relationships - Trustworthy leaders follow up on teams' concerns, give honest feedback, and resolve conflicts.

- Good judgment/expertise - Trustworthy leaders also use good judgment when making decisions, respond to problems quickly, and demonstrate their expertise.

- Consistency - Trustworthy leaders have integrity; they follow through on promises and their actions reflect their words.

These three factors are woven throughout this entire book, but consistency is particularly important with communication. We can all think of leaders who say one thing and do another.

Don't be that kind of leader.

Show up when you say you're going to show up. Hold a meeting when you say you're going to hold a meeting. Follow up when you say you're going to follow up. It's easy to drown in a list of to-dos and forget what you said you were going to do, so make friends with the reminder function on your phone and get good at acting on those reminders.

Take Action: Plan for Communication

You have two action steps for this chapter:

1. Prepare your Get-to-Know-You Survey for your back-to-school PD days. Buy a pack of index cards so that you can write down the top 10 challenges your team tells you about and keep them handy in your office.

2. Create your Remarkable Vision for your life, your family, and your school.

Chapter 3

Focus Your Efforts for Academic Impact

Remember playing Whac-a-Mole at the arcade when you were a kid? Armed with a soft pleather mallet, your goal was to smack down the plastic moles as they popped up randomly all over the mechanical game board. You could only win on pure adrenaline, whacking around at the board in a frenzy, hoping you were fast enough to put a stop to the madness.

As fun as it was, I think that game did us all a great disservice; it trained us to attack problems reactively in frantic spurts of adrenaline. We've learned to take action only when problems appear instead of seeking out long-term solutions by identifying the root of the problem.

Academics is the business of school. It's likely that when the new year starts (or even earlier), you will be overwhelmed with urgent academic issues. What's more—new urgent-feeling priorities and problems will arise throughout the year. Decisions will need to be made across a broad spectrum of academic concerns, including:

- Standardized testing

- Curriculum development

- Intervention and enrichment

- Acceleration

- MTSS

- RTI

- PLCs

- Grading

- And much, much more

Many of us have experienced what's often called initiative fatigue—the constant churn of projects and priorities as leaders react to the newest issues that come up during the year. Initiative fatigue is what happens when we're playing Whac-a-Mole with the academic needs across our school building.

As the leader, it's your job to stop this madness by bringing a more focused, thoughtful approach to setting academic priorities and establishing a process for academic improvement. Once you do that, then your job is to *trust your team*. So many leaders get addicted to the adrenaline rush of playing Whac-a-Mole that they find it hard to let go of the responsibility to be the ultimate problem-solver in their school.

News flash: You're not the only person who can make good decisions about how to serve your students. You're not the only person who can solve these sticky, complex problems. You need your team.

In this chapter, we'll talk about the four steps of instructional leadership that will get your academics off to a strong start this year: gather data, set goals, empower your team, and measure impact. These four steps will become a cycle that you can implement over and over again throughout the entire year.

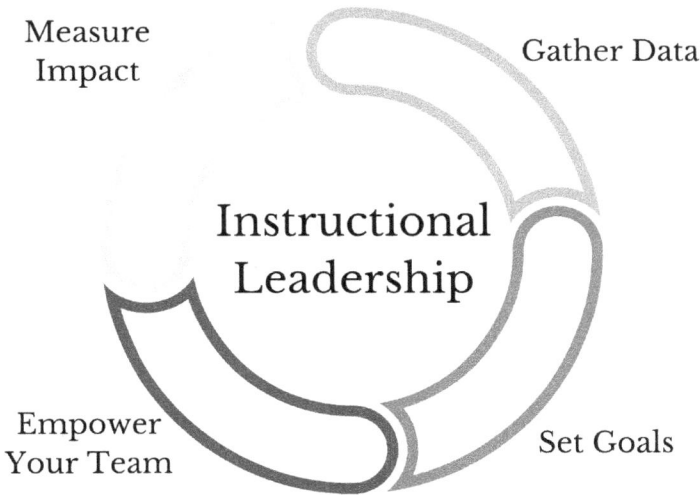

Measure Impact

Gather Data

Instructional Leadership

Empower Your Team

Set Goals

© Better Leaders Better Schools™, 2023

Gather Data

Hopefully you're picking up on a theme for these first 90 days: Listen first, act second. Before we can set goals or start to take any action, we have to get to know the students in our buildings and understand our school's academic strengths and weaknesses.

If you're a veteran leader or have been at your school for multiple years, it's likely that you already have a good sense of where the pain points are. New principals—whether new to administration in general or just new to a particular school—will need to spend more time listening and learning before setting priorities.

You'll want to collect annual standardized assessment data, formative assessment data across different departments and grade levels, and qualitative data such as surveys. (You'll already have one piece of qualitative data from the Get-to-Know-You Survey you'll be sending to your staff.)

I recommend empowering your department leads and grade-level or discipline-specific teams to not only gather relevant data, but to analyze it. Join as many of these meetings as you can, but let your teams take the lead.

First, teams should look at and discuss what's going well. Often, what your school is doing right isn't being celebrated like it should be. As you see things that merit celebration, make note to bring them up at the next PD meeting.

Next, teams should look for trends in the data to identify potential problem areas. Using disaggregated data can help schools spot the challenges for specific groups of students that may need additional support and attention.

After you've done your staff survey, consider conducting a similar Get-to-Know-You Student Survey as well. Relationships are the foundation of learning. All kids need to feel that at least one adult at the school cares about them, and you can get a sense for whether students in your building are feeling this way through a survey.

Below, I'm including some of my favorite questions to ask kids as a starting point, but you'll need to adjust this for your own student population. If you're serving elementary students, think about making an emoji survey or asking simple yes/no questions.

Alternatively, you can meet with students individually throughout the first 90 days to interview them personally.

Get-to-Know-You Student Survey

1. What do you want to know about your new principal?

2. What do you want me to know about you?

3. What is your favorite song and who performs it?

4. When is your birthday?

5. Share three of your favorite traditions at [Name of Your School].

6. Share the name of one teacher you know cares about you.

7. Share your top three strengths as a student.

8. How can I support you more at school?

9. If you were me, what would be your biggest priority?

Set Goals

Online biology teacher Leslie Samuel shares this analogy about impact: Imagine that you're trying to hammer through a piece of plywood. As you swing the hammer down, the force of the blow is strongest wherever the hammer hits, but it gets dispersed fairly quickly throughout the rest of the board. You might make only a dent in the wood.

Now imagine that you hold a sharp nail on top of the plywood and use the same amount of force to bring the hammer down onto the head of the nail. This time, the nail pierces through the wood with no problem because all of that force has been concentrated into a much smaller area. It took the same amount of effort, but the impact was much greater.

The same analogy applies to the priorities and initiatives we take on in school. When we try to apply our efforts to too many initiatives, we disperse our force and end up making small dents here and there. But when we focus our attention on just a few strategic priorities, we can maximize our impact.

The philosopher Seneca said something similar: "If a man knows not to which port he sails, no wind is favorable." This is why you'll want to pick no more than just three to five priorities to focus on per year.

Most leaders get this; it makes sense to us intuitively.

But that's not the hard part.

The hard part is sticking to those priorities throughout the year, even as other problems and issues rise to the surface. The temptation will be to start playing Whac-a-Mole again. You have to resist it, and you have to help your teams resist it. You simply don't have the mental capital, human resources, or time to tackle all of those problems. Taking on too much is the fastest path to a mediocre (or worse) school.

Obviously, there are going to be times when unavoidable problems come up. No one had "transition our entire school to distance learning" on their strategic priorities list at the start of the

2019–2020 school year—but a pandemic happened anyway, and we all had to adjust. There are certain issues that simply cannot be ignored. Thankfully, those are the exception, not the rule.

Learn to say *no* to even good opportunities so you can continue to say *yes* to what is most important.

The other constraint on your goal-setting is that you might not have the autonomy to choose all of your goals; sometimes certain priorities are set for you at the district level, and you have to work those in. But as you'll learn in Chapter 6, constraints can be powerful motivators for creativity.

Make sure that all of your department or grade-level teams agree on the priorities early on in the year. Then, as new problem areas arise, you can pause to ask:

- Have we solved our other priority problems yet?

- Should we de-prioritize another problem in order to focus on this new one?

Getting buy-in on the strategic focus right away will be critical to empowering your team to later take the appropriate action.

John Unger, the principal of West Fork Middle School, shared that one of the wins his team experienced from the five-day challenge was building a Response-to-Intervention (RTI) system throughout the building, starting with Tier 1 Positive Behavioral Interventions and Supports (PBIS). John's team modeled positive communication weekly to all of the staff, and soon, they saw that teachers followed suit, giving students handwritten notes offering encouragement and positive feedback.

The school had been trying to get an RTI system off the ground for years, and they were finally able to make it happen with the focus and clarity their 90-day entry plan gave them.

Empower Your Team

Your job as the instructional leader of your school is to lead your team's learning and then empower them with as much decision-making autonomy as you can to implement what they've learned.

Based on the feedback and data you've been gathering, you'll have set your priorities. Now is the time for you to prepare PD experiences throughout the year around those core areas. Identify your in-house experts and lean on them to help guide the rest of the team. Where you have gaps, consider hiring outside help to partner with internal team leads.

Invite your staff into the creation of a PD calendar for the year, and send that calendar out as early as possible so that your staff and teachers know what to expect. Check in with internal leads often to make sure they have what they need. After every PD meeting, send out a quick survey to invite feedback on what was discussed and make sure that you're staying committed to your strategic goals for the year.

Measure Impact

Project managers at companies typically look at two types of indicators to assess their progress: lead and lag indicators.

Lag indicators include information about the outcomes; they help identify where progress still needs to be made. Most leaders focus their energy here, which is a mistake. Lead indicators, on the other hand, refer to ideas that can help close the gap between where you are now and where you want to be. They are future-focused, action-oriented, and within your control.

Because lead indicators are within your control, they are what matters most. If the right actions are taken, the outcomes will happen anyway.

Progress trumps performance every day.

Finally, don't forget to measure the intangibles. You can do this in your after-PD surveys, during classroom visits, and via individual check-ins with staff. How much joy and investment do you see in your team? Are they happy to show up to work everyday?

Remember, often the smallest details can make the biggest impact on your school's culture. That's what we'll discuss in Chapter 4.

Take Action: Plan for PD

You have two action steps for this chapter:

1. Start collecting any quantitative data available to you, like grades and standardized testing scores.

2. If you already know your team, start identifying your in-house experts who might be willing to lead PD throughout the year.

Chapter 4

Co-Create an Extraordinary Culture

In his book, *The Promises of Giants*, author and business psychologist John Amaechi (2021) tells a potent story about the importance of culture. The story is about the residents who live in an apartment building where all of their apartments border a shared common area.

Some of the residents smoke. When they are done with a cigarette, they flick the butts onto the ground.

"Someone else will pick them up," they say.

Other residents start to notice the trash in the common area. *Not my problem*, they think. After all, it isn't their cigarette butt. But now those residents start to leave behind sandwich wrappers, water bottles, paper, and plastic bags.

"Someone else will pick them up," they say.

Next come the cardboard boxes. Finally, a mattress is abandoned.

The garbage continues to pile up, yet no one does anything about it.

The smokers continue to smoke, flicking their cigarette butts onto the ground, until one day, the embers catch on the cardboard, which sets fire to the rest of the litter. The whole thing goes up in flames, endangering the entire apartment complex.

What was once a problem that no one took responsibility for is now everyone's problem.

Everyone is responsible for the culture of an organization, too. And what is a culture? It's the accumulation of our choices. John Amaechi (2018) writes, "People make choices. Choices make culture."

It usually starts with something small. We notice that someone's actions or words aren't aligned with our mission, but we let it slide. *Not my problem*, we think. We notice that our colleagues are passing off responsibilities like a hot potato. But hey—not our problem.

As a leader, it's tempting to want to keep the peace or ignore potential culture issues that aren't really problems yet. We have too many other things on our plate.

This strategy works fine until one day, you've got a fire on your hands. Suddenly, that toxic culture has become everyone's problem—especially yours.

Why We Ignore Culture

"Fires" and emergencies are the most common reasons I hear leaders give for losing focus on their school's culture. They're busy, and they have lots of urgent problems to address. Without even realizing it, culture gets pushed to the side.

The other obstacle to nurturing our culture is administrivia: paperwork, tasks, to-do lists. There are constant inputs and demands on your time that all take your attention away from culture.

You can't afford to let that happen.

Culture is the heartbeat of your school. It's especially important in the first 90 days because those days set a precedent for the rest of the year. In this chapter, I'll share some of my favorite ways to make culture a priority in your school.

Take the Temperature

How do you know what your school's current culture is in the first place—especially if you're a new leader or new to the school? Sometimes it's difficult for leaders to get an accurate read on how people really feel.

To help make it easier for everyone to share their thoughts, I like to use the following exercise in a staff meeting. You can repeat this a few times throughout the year to help you stay up-to-date, and you can try it with students and parents, too.

- First, find at least 10 random pictures that evoke strong

emotions. For example:

- One of your students

- Puppy

- Older person

- Nature

- Space

- Traffic jam

- Paperwork

- Ask staff to sort the pictures and pick the top three that best represent the quality of your school culture.

- Ask for volunteers to explain their reasoning, or if there's time, let everyone share their thoughts.

- How do their responses align with the Remarkable School Vision you developed in Chapter 2?

This activity will help you understand the cultural history of the school and identify potential issues.

Put Relationships First

Quality relationships lead to a quality culture, and vice versa. As the leader of your organization, you set the tone and example for everyone else. The time and energy you put into building relationships will pay dividends in improving your school's culture.

Be Present

The best place to begin is by staying present during interactions with our staff. This is often difficult! We're so attuned to looking out for problems and staying on top of the demands of administrivia that it can be hard to set those aside. And yet, the number one way to show people we care is by honoring them with our full attention.

The self-care you've been practicing will come in handy here. It's hard to be fully invested in others when your back hurts, you didn't sleep well, or you're starving. Practicing mindfulness will train your brain to stop being so reactive to the constant interruptions coming your way.

Create a Culture Team

Remember, culture is everyone's responsibility, not just yours. Create a team of culture ambassadors in your school. This team might include staff, students, parents, and other stakeholders. They will be your culture cheerleaders and help you to represent the school's vision throughout the community.

Get Explicit About Belonging and Othering

School culture is about our choices, but more specifically, it's about the impact our choices have on everyone else in the school community. It's about how we make others *feel*.

In the first 90 days, you can establish a common language around culture by talking specifically about both belonging and othering. Belonging is about the way we create a welcoming and inclusive environment where everyone feels valued, whereas othering is about the ways we (intentionally or unintentionally) exclude and separate people within our organization.

To get this conversation started, lead your team through this exercise:

- In the middle of a whiteboard, write the question: How does belonging feel?

- Give everyone five to 10 minutes to discuss. Consider playing some of their favorite songs from the Get-to-Know-You Survey in the background.

- Next, invite everyone to share, and as they do, create a mindmap on a whiteboard. You'll probably hear words and phrases like safe, trusted, connected, or making a contribution.

- Have someone from your culture team take a picture of these words as a snapshot of how everyone can create a culture of belonging.

- Then, write the next question on the board: How does othering feel?

- Again, take five to 10 minutes to discuss. Othering might feel like being invisible, isolated, diminished, or unwelcome.

- Take another picture of these insights as a reminder of the feelings and emotions to look out for. They are the cigarette butts and garbage that piles up over time.

- Refer back to your mindmap work throughout the year.

If you invest in forms of belonging and work to eradicate the ways people feel othered in your organization, the quality of both your relationships and culture will improve.

Create Moments

Once, I was coaching an elementary school leader who wanted help improving her school's culture. The school was heavily invested in PLCs and loved data. This principal was so excited about the gains her Tier-3 intervention teachers were making and had been celebrating their success. Unfortunately, she'd received feedback that the rest of the staff felt overlooked since their progress wasn't as dramatic as the Tier-3 teachers'.

This leader had done a great job recognizing and celebrating one group of teachers but needed to find ways to recognize and celebrate everyone's accomplishments.

We do that by creating moments.

Author Chip Heath (2017) writes, "Moments are what we remember and what we cherish. Certainly we might celebrate achieving a goal, such as completing a marathon or landing a significant client—but the achievement is embedded in a moment. [...] This is what we mean by 'thinking in moments': to recognize where the prose of life needs punctuation."

Remember my sticky core value about the purple cow from Chapter 1? Creating moments is how I live out this value in my work everyday.

Some obvious moments for your school are the first day, holidays, and the end of a quarter or semester—but you don't have to wait for a milestone to create moments. Let's talk about how to do this regularly throughout the school year.

Consistent Celebration

When I was a principal, my culture team sent out a Staff Member of the Month nomination form to all students, faculty, and parents. This form listed every staff member in the school, including the bus drivers and the staff who served lunch everyday, all of the teachers and custodians, and finally, our vice principal and myself.

The person filling out the form would check one person's name from the list. Then, the form listed our school's core values, and the person would check the core value the nominee best exhibited. The final two questions were:

- How does this person live out this core value?

- Anything else you want us to know?

The culture team compiled the results and awarded one prize to a stand-out staff member every month. They made sure that these prizes were awarded equitably throughout the year.

But what's more—even those who didn't "win" still received a copy of the nominations they received so that they could see the positive feedback and compliments that others had written about them. Those forms were not anonymous, so they could follow up with the person who nominated them to thank them.

This monthly ritual was such a hit and staff were so excited about the feedback they received that they took to posting their nomination forms in the staff lounge every month. It was a great lesson for me on the power of moments.

Remember That You Set the Tone

Author Todd Whitaker (2011) writes, "When the principal sneezes, the whole school catches a cold" (p. 36).

Just as teachers set the tone in their classrooms, you set the tone for the whole school. Staying present and engaged, putting relationships first, and buying into the magic of moments begins with you.

Take Action: Gather Your Culture Team

You have two action steps for this chapter:

1. Create a culture team at your school.

2. Plan to lead one or both of the exercises listed in this chapter—or empower your culture team to do so.

Chapter 5

Pare Down to Scale Up Operations

When leaders start thinking about how to plan for a new school year, they usually think of operations first. That's why I've saved it for last—because we have to plan for the important before the urgent.

Now that we've done that, let's talk about how to handle the urgent.

It's probably not hard for you to think of all of the operational challenges facing you: onboarding new faculty, welcoming students and families, establishing policies and managing district mandates, filing reports, creating the master schedule, and maintaining the facilities—just to start.

Three principles will help to guide us as we tackle the quickly-growing to-do list.

Less Is More

In 1960, Random House founder Bennett Cerf challenged one of his most famous authors to a bet: Write an entire book using just 50 words. The prize: $50.

That author was Theodor Geisel, aka Dr. Seuss.

The book born out of this dare became his most beloved children's book, *Green Eggs and Ham*, and it has sold over 200 million copies to date.

The surprising and profitable lesson from this little experiment was that less is more. The greater the constraint, the greater the creativity required. With only 50 words at his disposal, Dr. Seuss had to access his creativity in a new way, and it led to a breakthrough.

What's even more remarkable is that 49 of the words he used only had one syllable! The 50th had three: anywhere.

Dr. Seuss liked this strategy of using constraints so much that he employed it in all of his future books, too (Clear, n.d.).

While handling operations can feel like a chore, we can access greater creativity—perhaps even make it fun—by establishing constraints for ourselves. Constraints work because they force us to boil the task down to its most essential elements and change the way we perceive what we're actually trying to accomplish. They help us shed the weight of "the way we've always done things."

French writer and aviator Antoine de Saint-Exupéry (1939) knew the power of distilling an idea or a task to its most fundamental levels: "It seems that perfection is achieved not when there is nothing more to add, but when there is nothing more to take away" (p. 59).

Dedicate just one hour per day to handling operations-related issues, or set aggressive deadlines for operations tasks. In his blog, James Clear (n.d.) describes how he commits to a schedule for writing articles ahead of time, and it's forced him to get creative with finding time for writing: "Constraints force you to get something done and don't allow you to procrastinate. This is why I believe that professionals set a schedule for their production while amateurs wait until they feel motivated."

Delegate

You already know that I believe in trusting and empowering your team. Along with the academic priorities, we can also learn to trust our team to take on operational tasks or handle the "fires" that so often seem to come up.

Sometimes what we think are emergencies are really just distractions. Often, our pride and ego as the leader make us think we need to be involved in everything when in reality, our team might be just as (or even more) qualified to handle certain things so that we can keep the focus on our academic priorities and culture.

Delegating doesn't diminish your impact; it actually multiplies it.

When delegating, you can define the boundaries and constraints of the task or project. You can establish processes and set expectations around when you want to be contacted. You know your people's strengths and can tap into their passions and excitement. You get to give them decision-making autonomy and authority; you can empower them to show off their leadership skills.

This is a hard shift for many leaders who have been used to overperforming, taking on too much, and trying to manage everything themselves. They wonder, *What role is left for me if I am delegating well to my team?*

Their role is to provide direction and coaching. Their role is also to clear the path, provide resources, and recognize their team's effort.

To help you decide what tasks are right to delegate, create a spreadsheet or table with five columns:

Tasks	Hell Yeah or Hell Nah	Keep, Delegate, Eliminate?	Next Steps	Deadline

You can create your own spreadsheet or use the one I've created for you at buildleadershipmomentum.com.

Aim to give away a minimum of three operational tasks per quarter or a maximum of three tasks per month. Communicate intentionally about any expectations you have around the project, and check in with your team regularly to see what else they need from you in order to be successful.

I've also created a Delegation Masterclass that goes into more depth about when and how to delegate effectively. You can access that class via our website: buildleadershipmomentum.com.

Keep Score

Now, I don't mean keep score against your colleagues or create competition among them.

The only person you should be keeping score with is *yourself*.

As you already know, there's a lot to accomplish in the first 90 days of school. Even your 90-day plan, which we'll create in Chapter 6, will cover a lot of detail on every aspect we've covered so far: yourself, communication, academics, school culture, and operations. You'll need an easy way to measure your progress.

The best way to do this is to set your main priority for each day. Keeping track is easy: Just write your priority in your planner or set a reminder on your phone, and then check it off as you complete it. Every single day, Monday through Friday, you should have the potential to score a 5 out of 5 for the week.

Don't calculate your score daily! Worrying about keeping score daily might distract you from your work or set too rigid a boundary. At the end of the week or month, add up what you've accomplished and divide it by the total number of tasks you set for yourself. As long as you're scoring 80 percent or higher, you're doing great.

Are you ready to turn the page to actually create your plan? You now have everything you need for a successful first 90 days of school.

Now, let's get started.

Take Action: Get Your Tasks in Order

You have four action steps for this chapter:

1. Create a list of all of the operational tasks you can think of that you'll need to accomplish in the first 90 days.

2. Download the delegation spreadsheet I created or create your own, and then fill it out.

3. For each task, identify the constraints and deadlines.

4. Communicate with your team about what they can take on and what you will keep.

Chapter 6

Build Your Perfect 90-Day Entry Plan

Remember your vision for Day 91 that you wrote down in Chapter 1?

Go back to it now that you've read more about each of the five buckets, and revise it to include new ideas you've learned. Your hopes for how your school will make people feel might be the same, but ideally, you now have more specific actions and ideas to add to it.

In this chapter, we're going to talk about how to make that vision a reality.

Pacing Your 90-Day Entry Plan

If you try to tackle all five buckets at full speed every day for the first 90 days, you will burn out long before Thanksgiving. Instead, you need to divide those 90 days into meaningful and strategic checkpoints that you'll be building your plan around:

- Before school starts

- Day 1

- Week 1

- Month 1

- Month 2

- Month 3

At each of these strategic checkpoints, you'll be asking yourself:

- What do I want to accomplish in this time period?

- What aspects of the five buckets am I implementing?

- How will I communicate this focus to everyone in the school?

- How will I keep score and measure progress?

This new scaffolding might be an adjustment from what you're used to. John Unger, principal at West Fork Middle School, shared that at first, it was difficult for him to envision what school should look like 60 or 90 days out—but by starting with specific actions before school started and scaffolding up from there, he was able to scale each of the five buckets seamlessly and communicate the new vision to his team in a way that made sense for everyone.

A Model for Your Perfect Entry Plan

The following is a model for what your 90-day action plan could look like. It's filled with the ideas and activities for each bucket that we discussed in previous chapters—but go crazy with it! Make a ruckus and change it to fit your needs.

To make it easier for you, I've created a blank template that you can download at buildleadershipmomentum.com.

BEFORE SCHOOL STARTS: SET THE STAGE

You	▶ Fill out the Ruckus Maker Mindset Tool™ and identify areas you want to grow in.
Communications	▶ Create your Get-to-Know-You Survey.
Academics	▶ Find out the district's preexisting expectations/goals. ▶ Gather any quantitative data that is available to you (e.g., standardized test scores, grades, etc.).
Culture	▶ During an in-service day, do the 10-picture activity from Chapter 4 to take the temperature of your school's culture.
Operations	▶ Identify the operational needs that will have to be accomplished in the first day/week of school. ▶ Make a plan to keep score on the operational tasks you want to accomplish each day, and set reminders in your phone.

FIRST DAY OF SCHOOL

You	▶ How do you plan to incorporate eating, sleeping, meditating, moving, and unplugging on the first day? ▶ How can you integrate something fun and unique to you with your first day plans?
Communications	▶ Be visible. ▶ Make a point to welcome everybody individually. ▶ Visit classrooms. ▶ Check in with staff ahead of time to make sure everyone has the information they need to succeed on Day 1.
Academics	▶ While visiting classrooms, look for one good thing about the quality of the teacher's instruction in each classroom. ▶ Leave each teacher a message sharing what you noticed.
Culture	▶ Make this day a powerful moment and celebrate it.
Operations	▶ Be available and visible so you can help with any "fires" that arise.

WEEK 1: FOCUS ON RELATIONSHIPS

You	▶ How do you plan to incorporate eating, sleeping, meditating, moving, and unplugging throughout your week? ▶ How can you share something meaningful from your life with your staff?
Communications	▶ Create the Get-to-Know-You Survey during PD. (Alternatively, complete before school starts.) ▶ Take note of common challenges and write them on index cards.
Academics	▶ Continue visiting classrooms and finding one good thing to praise staff for. Try to visit all classrooms, counseling spaces, the cafeteria, and so on by the end of the week. ▶ Send out Get-to-Know-You Student Surveys or meet with students to interview them personally.
Culture	▶ Conduct the Belonging and Othering Exercise during one of your first PD gatherings.
Operations	▶ Refine your scoring system. Does it work, or are there any tweaks you want to make in how you keep score? ▶ Start compiling a long-term list of operational tasks that need to be accomplished.

MONTH 1: TAKE IT ALL IN

You	▶ Set goals for eating, sleeping, meditating, moving, and unplugging for the whole month. ▶ Pick someone to be accountable to and share your goals with them. Ask them to follow up throughout the month. ▶ What specific ways can you share more about yourself with your staff and learn more about them?
Communications	▶ Ask your administrative assistant to schedule 15-minute individual meetings with your staff throughout the month so you can get to know them and follow up on their survey responses. ▶ Refine what you identified as top challenges on the index cards as you learn more. ▶ Identify a rhythm or schedule for communicating consistently through multiple channels.
Academics	▶ Identify your in-house experts in different instructional areas. ▶ With your in-house experts, co-create a PD calendar for the rest of the year. ▶ As academic challnges arise, take action that delivers quick wins.
Culture	▶ Gather a culture team. ▶ Have your culture team take the lead on identifying your school's sticky core values. ▶ Make powerful moments: Identify important dates and milestones in your school's calendar.
Operations	▶ Download the delegation spreadsheet and start asking your staff to take on certain tasks. ▶ Add up your score for this month. Are you hitting 80 percent or higher?

MONTH 2: VISION & GOALS

You	▶ Complete the Ruckus Maker Mindset Tool™ again. How are you measuring up against the first time you completed it? ▶ Set new goals for eating, sleeping, meditating, moving, and unplugging for the whole month. ▶ Pick someone to be accountable to and share your goals with them. Commit to when you will check in. ▶ What specific ways can you share more about yourself with your staff and learn more about them?
Communications	▶ Draft your Remarkable School Vision and invite feedback from your leadership team. ▶ Are you still communicating consistently in the channels you identified?
Academics	▶ Review and analyze data. ▶ At a staff meeting, present the long-term challenges you've identified and invite staff to help make an action plan to address them. ▶ Set goals together.
Culture	▶ Kick off the Staff Member of the Month nominations. ▶ Celebrate any powerful moments in your school calendar.
Operations	▶ How many tasks have you given away? Aim to give away a minimum of three operational tasks per quarter or a maximum of three tasks per month. ▶ Add up your score for this month. Are you hitting 80 percent or higher?

MONTH 3: PROGRESS & PLANNING

You	▶ Complete the Ruckus Maker Mindset Tool™ again. How are you measuring up this month? ▶ Set new goals for eating, sleeping, meditating, moving, and unplugging for the whole month. ▶ Continue your agreed upon check-in schedule with your accountability partner. ▶ What specific ways can you share more about yourself with your staff and learn more about them?
Communications	▶ After receiving and implementing feedback from your leadership team on your Remarkable School Vision, send it to department heads and other leaders throughout the school to gather feedback from their teams as well. ▶ Are you still communicating consistently in the channels you identified? ▶ Seek feedback from your staff: Is your communication meeting their needs?
Academics	▶ Identify lead indicators: What will you measure to make progress towards your goals? ▶ Check in with your team to see how you can support them in making decisions and progress.
Culture	▶ Celebrate any powerful moments in your school calendar. ▶ Make plans to celebrate the 100th day of school.
Operations	▶ How many tasks have you given away? Aim to give away a minimum of three operational tasks per quarter or a maximum of three tasks per month. ▶ Add up your score for this month. Are you hitting 80 percent or higher?

Completing Your Entry Plan

Don't complete your action plan alone. Like Principal John Unger, you can join the Ruckus Maker Nation through our website, buildleadershipmomentum.com, to find support and encouragement, and you can even join our next challenge. John said he enjoyed the collaborative environment and meeting other principals and school leaders across the world to give him ideas and find solidarity.

Once you have a draft of your plan, if you haven't already, bring in your leadership team to help revise it and make changes before you start implementing.

Even then, your action plan is not going to be perfect, and it should never be "done." It'll need polishing throughout the first 90 days. Keeping in mind the quote from Antoine de Saint-Exupery, remove as much as you can to maintain your focus and clarity about what you want to accomplish in each bucket.

John shared that his team used a simple cycle of inquiry to continuously refine their plan:

- Plan

- Do

- Reflect

As they came across new challenges, they were able to make adjustments while still maintaining their overall focus on their goals for each of the five buckets.

The other advice I give to leaders as they start to roll out their plan is this: Don't stress about bad days! At some point, something will go wrong. Expect it. Embrace it. Stay focused on the big goals and begin again.

And here's the best part about the 90-day action plan: It's not just for the first 90 days!

You can use this template to plan not just for back to school, but for every quarter of the school year.

The Impact Is Worth the Effort

When I asked John what it was like implementing his first 90-day entry plan, he said, "Honestly, that stress was completely gone."

Besides the positive weekly communication, the successful launch of their RTI system, and the creation of the West Fork family engagement committee, John says that they've been able to create a culture of belonging throughout the school, and he's increased the leadership capacity in his team by delegating and building trust.

And they haven't stopped there; now, his team uses the 90-day entry plan to guide their focus throughout the entire school year.

Completing the action plan takes some dedicated time, but John and the other principals who have implemented their plans feel the effort is well worth it. "It's an investment, but it pays off," John said. "Are you willing to give up 10 to 20 hours of planning for a successful school year?"

That's a great question. How will you answer it?

John and other principals like him have learned that a 90-day entry plan is a gift to their communities. It takes planning and a commitment to listening and learning, to pausing and reflecting, to focusing and pruning, and to including and welcoming. But the payoff is a greater positive impact on each of the five buckets in your school, and forward momentum to carry you through the rest of the school year.

Most of all, it takes a commitment to yourself. Will *you* be the kind of principal who gives your best self to your school?

Are you willing, Ruckus Maker?

Level Up Your Leadership

We all know that the best gift we can give to our schools is our best selves. Reading a book is a great start toward that goal—but it's just that: a *start*.

How do you continue to grow and evolve as a leader? How do you level up your learning to become the ultimate Ruckus Maker?

Relevant, Responsive, and Results-Oriented Professional Development™

In 2015, I had two problems as a new administrator.

Problem 1: The professional development I experienced was Too Little Too Late, Unhelpful, and Disconnected.

Problem 2: Leadership "development" only talked about academics, attendance, and discipline. All important, just not *why* I got into education.

So I eventually joined my first mastermind to grow my skills and impact. And then a lightbulb went off in my head.

What if there were other Ruckus Makers just like me out there? Leaders who wanted to experience professional development that was Relevant, Responsive, and Results-Oriented.

And what if I launched a mastermind for *those* Ruckus Makers in education?

So I did.

Our community has grown over the years from the seven early adopters to 80 strong in nine cohorts around the world (We even have a cohort focused on Africa/Europe/Middle East.).

Then, in 2019, Corwin reached out and asked me to do a book about how we serve school leaders through the structure of a mastermind. Corwin noticed that we were supporting leaders in a new and different way.

The first draft of *Mastermind* was rotten. I had to actually stop writing the book in order to write a better book.

So I spent hours walking with my dog, Alba, in Syracuse's Barry Park. And in Barry Park, I thought, *What is the framework that makes the mastermind work?*

Finally, I got it.

The mastermind works because we intentionally integrate Authenticity, Belonging, and Challenge. That's what I call the ABCs of Powerful Professional Development®.

Ever since that realization, the mastermind and the ABCs have been changing the landscape of PD for school leaders.

To date, John Unger and dozens of principals like him have joined the mastermind, and there is always—*always*—room for more.

Want to join us? We'd love to see you there.

Learn more at
https://betterleadersbetterschools.com/mastermind.

Online Resources

Access all of the resources mentioned throughout this book and listed below (and more!) at our online portal: buildleadershipmomentum.com.

Chapter 1: Bring Your Best Self to School

- The Ruckus Maker Mindset Tool

Chapter 2: Communicate How Much You Care

- Bonus Section: Why Communicate?

- Get-to-Know-You Survey Questions

Chapter 3: Focus Your Efforts for Academic Impact

- Get-to-Know-You Student Survey

Chapter 4: Co-Create an Extraordinary Culture

- Activity: Take the Temperature

- Activity: Belonging and Othering

- Staff Member of the Month Nomination Form

Chapter 5: Pare Down to Scale Up Operations

- Delegation Spreadsheet

- Delegation Masterclass

Chapter 6: Build Your Perfect 90-Day Entry Plan

- 90-Day Entry Plan Template

- The Ruckus Maker Nation Online Community

References

Amaechi, J. [@JohnAmaechi]. (2018, January 1). *People make choices. Choices make culture. Make - and help others make - better choices in 2018* [Image attached] [Tweet]. Twitter. https://twitter.com/JohnAmaechi/status/947955349293817856

Clear, J. (n.d.). The weird strategy Dr. Seuss used to create his greatest work. https://jamesclear.com/dr-seuss

de Saint-Exupéry, A. (1939). *Terre de hommes* [Land of men]. Le Livre de Poche.

Godin, S. (2004). *Purple cow: Transform your business by being remarkable.* Gardners Books.

Haden, J. (2020, December 29). Exceptional performers like Hugh Jackman and Usain Bolt follow the 85 percent rule. So should you. *Inc.* https://www.inc.com/jeff-haden/optimal-performers-like-hugh-jackman-usain-bolt-follow-85-percent-rule-so-should-you.html

Heath, C., & Heath, D. (2017). *The power of moments: Why certain experiences have extraordinary impact.* Simon & Schuster.

Hiatt, B. (2018, February 20). Husband finds Laverton school principal Tish Antulov dead at her desk. *The West Australian.* https://www.perthnow.com.au/news/wa/husband-finds-laverton-school-principal-trish-antulov-dead-at-her-desk-ng-b88751673z

Salciccioli, G. (2011). *The enemies of excellence growth guide.* https://f.hubspotusercontent00.net/hubfs/5535000/Enemies%20 of%20Excellence_Website%20Tools/Enemies%20of%20Excellenc e_Growth%20Guide.pdf

Sinek, S. (2014). *Leaders eat last.* Portfolio.

Steiner, E. D., Doan, S., Woo, A., Gittens, A. D., Lawrence, R. A., Berdie, L., Wolfe, R. L., Greer, L., & Schwartz, H. L. (2022). Restoring teacher and principal well-being is an essential step for rebuilding schools: Findings from the state of the American teacher and state of the American principal surveys. *RAND Corporation.* https://www.rand.org/pubs/research_reports/RRA1108-4.html

Sullivan, E. T. (2022, July 6). Principals are on the brink of a breakdown. *EdSurge.*

Weiner, J. (2020, September 3). *Jeff Weiner on leading like a CEO* [Video]. LinkedIn. https://www.linkedin.com/learning/jeff-weiner-on-leading-like-a -ceo/effectively-communicating-repetition?autoplay=true

Whitaker, T. (2011). *What great principals do differently: Eighteen things that matter most.* Routledge.

Zenger, J., & Folkman, J. (2019, February 5). The 3 elements of trust. *Harvard Business Review.* https://hbr.org/2019/02/the-3-elements-of-trust

www.ingramcontent.com/pod-product-compliance
Lightning Source LLC
Chambersburg PA
CBHW070027030426
42335CB00017B/2327